Joseph Scheer

Night Visions

The Secret Designs of Moths

Prestel
Munich · Berlin · London · New York

Contents

Attracted to Light

Joseph Scheer

Understanding things through images has always been part of my work. How we believe things reveal themselves to us and how we try to order them to make sense of the world around us has also been of great interest to me. Complex meanings can be drawn from what at first may seem a simple image. Can something as basic as the image of a common moth reveal things we know or do not quite know about our current culture and ourselves? For me, all such revelations are likely and this possibility attracts me to moths as they are in turn attracted to light. The wide variety of symbolisms of and metaphors related to moths are a source of great curiosity. For most people they probably carry more negative connotations than positive ones. Moths generate familiar reactions related to common complaints about eaten clothes, contaminated food, and senseless acts of self-immolation. These creatures that tend to favor the night are often given second-rate status in relation to the "beautiful" butterflies of the sunlit day. My exploration of moths, however, has led me to draw other conclusions.

Moths outnumber butterflies 8 to 1, are far more diverse, and have their own unique kind of beauty. Not all moths come readily to light and quite a few species are only on the wing during the day, but a great majority of them cannot resist many forms of bright light during evening hours. These can be porch lights or even the monitor screen of my computer with which a large *Polyphemus* (pl. 16) once collided after flying in through an open window.

Plusia putnami

Soon after the newly formed Institute for Electronic Arts received its first high-resolution scanner from Scitex (now Creo Corporation) its technician came and calibrated it and pronounced it "ready to do a scan". As there was a small gnat flying around a plant near the scanner, I quickly grabbed it, threw it onto the new device, and proceeded to scan it at maximum resolution. When the scan was finished and I opened the file on the computer, what I saw was incredible. This little creature had metallic pearlescent wings, hairs all over its tiny body and two beautiful, multi-faceted compound eyes. I never had looked at a gnat before with any interest, dismissing them as minor nuisances, unworthy of my attention. This experience opened a whole new world for me. I became aware of the complexity of the many insects surrounding us all the time. I began to think of the many things buzzing by or crawling around my feet in the vegetation as I walked down the street.

Along with the scanner, the Institute also received an Iris printer. Originally designed as a commercial color-proofing device, it had become a much sought-after printer for artists working in digital media when they discovered it could print on a variety of papers beyond the commercial proofing ones for which it was intended. A printmaker by training, I have always used a variety of hand-made papers from around the world for my work. The Iris could produce excellent images on these papers with rich saturated color and exquisite detail. With the Scitex scanner and Iris printer coupled together, the Institute now had some very powerful tools for artists to use.

I was truly impressed with the magnificent image of a gnat that my new tools had helped me create. I wanted to explore more insects in the same way and reveal their fabulous intricacies in magnified images. The Iris printer can create large-scale prints up to 86 x 117 centimeters. I thought I should try to capture numerous insect images for a possible gallery installation where prints could be clustered together on the walls. At this point it was early spring and I had done a number of tests on various insects that I had found lying at the bottom of windows in several art studios at the school where I teach. They were not in the best shape and had dried in random positions. Although most of these were species of flies, wasps, and bees, there were also numerous moths among them.

I thought that if I worked really hard I could collect perhaps 200 different species by the end of summer from which I could choose to make prints. As an artist/printmaker whose work was crossing over into new media I had only modest technical training in the natural sciences but was greatly interested in the field. I got a few books on insects, collected the necessary supplies, and began my hunt in earnest. Not worrying too much about how ridiculous I looked running around with a butterfly net, I quickly became quite skilled at catching all sorts of insects. After just two weeks, I had collected what I estimated to be well over the 200 species that I had thought would take the entire summer to gather. These included flying ants, beetles, damselflies, mayflies, dragonflies, stoneflies, gnats, midges, mosquitoes, butterflies, true bugs, bees, wasps, hornets, horseflies, and moths.

I scanned my entire catch and started to produce prints. Even though many of the images were amazing, it seemed to be all too disparate to make sense. It also seemed too easy and random: now that I was beginning to do research on insect species, I realized what a ridiculously low number 200 was. It would not have been any less ridiculous if I had chosen 2000 as my goal since even that would not have registered a dent in the insect order.

Trichotaphe flavocostella

Moths, I thought, constituted the most intriguing section of my small collection. I had been aware of them over the years and had kept a saucer on my desk for ones that had flown into the Art Building during the summer months and died on the floor near windows. I had previously tried to use them in prints and incorporate them in video, but was never really happy with the results. The scans and prints that I was now able to create, with all their amazing details, were revealing a great deal of visual information about these creatures. The symbolism of moths, together with what I was starting to realize about their diversity, became more significant. Their species diversity was demonstrated in the many distinctive antennae, elaborate patterns, and the shapes of their wings. Some appeared to be hirsute, such as moths from the family Lasiocampidae, while others were every bit as colorful and elegant as any butterfly. Some, such as the family Sesiidae, mimicked wasps while plume moths (pls. 57, 58, 59) rolled their wing at rest and could easily be mistaken for crane flies. The sheer number of species surprised me. I stopped collecting other insects and began to focus solely on moths.

My friend and colleague Mark Klingensmith was building a house on a hundred acres of land outside the reach of light pollution, so this location seemed like the ideal collector's site. Mark, the technical specialist for the Institute for Electronic Arts, is also, along with his wife Kasey, an accomplished organic gardener and they have planted numerous varieties of heirloom vegetables, herbs and flowers. They do not use pesticides, so the gardens are a source of food that supports the diversity of local species. For example, each summer the hummingbird clearwing moth, *Hemaris thysbe* (pl. 7), visits the bergamot flowers.

We set up three relatively permanent trap areas, each consisting of a light source behind a white translucent sheet, to attract the moths. We also use a couple of mobile lights that can be moved to different locations. Our new goal was to try to capture and scan at least one specimen from each species of moth that lives at this location. Capturing moths became a nightly ritual that has gone on during warm weather months for five straight years and will continue for many more. Beyond fixing the electronic tools when they malfunction, Mark has been an active participant in the project collecting specimens, building light traps, and recording sound and video for future exhibitions.

Actias luna

With approximately 1000 species encountered so far I am beginning to realize how complex and diverse the moth population is in our area. Moreover, the population is not constant: in any given location the diversity of species remains in flux. As many as 500 moths of *Noctua pronuba*, a recent arrival to North America, (pl. 31) may appear in one night. Another species, the metallic green *Diachrysia balluca*, has never shown up more then once or twice during entire summers, or has been totally absent in others. The first year we began collecting, there was a burst in the population of both *Ctenucha virginica* (pl. 33) and *Halysidota tessellaris* (pl. 23). There were hundreds of them on the sheets every night in early summer when they tend to emerge. In the summers since then they have still made their appearance as a species, but only in modest numbers of ten or so per evening. There appears to be a natural ebb and flow to the population of moth species.

The weather and the moon greatly affect what will be attracted to our lights. In our part of the country moths start flying as soon as the temperature rises above 50 degrees Fahrenheit. New moons and cloudy nights are significantly better for moth collection than full moons and clear nights. A warm cloudy night with a slight drizzle of rain appears to generate the best conditions for attracting the largest number of moths to our lights.

In our region with its shorter Northern growing season the majority of moth species produce only one generation. Species with a single generation emerge from early spring to the end of November. This often relates to how the moths over-winter. The majority of species that emerge in spring through early summer have caterpillars that develop fully and over-winter in the pupal state. The moths that emerge in late summer and through the fall, as in the genus *Catocala*, lay eggs that over-winter and then hatch in early spring, reaching pupal and adult stages during the warmer months. The family Arctiidae has many species whose caterpillars over-winter. Some of these caterpillars are known as "woolly bears" and include some of the most colorful of all moths such as *Grammia virgo* (pl. 18), *Arctia caja americana* (pl. 22) and *Pyrrharctia isabella*. The caterpillar of the last moth is credited in folklore with predicting the severity of winter depending on the ratio of orange to black in its coloring. The moths that emerge in late fall often over-winter as adults, and a number of species that

are seen during the last few warm days of early November will be seen again in March and April. Mark often finds them in his sap buckets when he taps his sugar maples for syrup in February with a blanket of snow still on the ground!

In mid-spring the giant silk moths, the Saturniidae, are on the wing. One of the most spectacular among them is the Luna moth, *Actias luna* (pl. 9). The sight of these emerald-colored long-tailed creatures in flight is quite magical to behold. The Luna has appeared each year in healthy numbers along with other species of saturniids with the exception of the Cecropia moth. We have seen only three individuals of *Hyalophora cecropia* (pl. 17), two of those during the same year. It is the largest of all moths in our area with a wingspan of over 15 centimeters. I have read a number of articles about the decline of this species that link it to the recent measures for the control of the Gypsy moth. Non-native parasitic wasps and flies that were introduced to control Gypsy moth caterpillars also attack Cecropia caterpillars. There are concerns that this intervention could be the reason behind a possible decline of the Cecropias.

Smerinthus jamaicensis

Another family that starts flying in spring, but reaches its peak in early summer is the Notodontidae, also known as the Prominents. Some rest with their wings folded, tent-like, over their bodies (*Nadata gibbosa*, pl. 29) while the species of *Schizura* (pl. 39) roll their wings and stick almost straight up like large buds or small twigs on a branch. The Notodontidae are often described as "drab colored," mostly gray or brown, but after having scanned almost thirty species in this family, I cannot agree. Once they are enlarged to reveal every scale their multitudinous colors are revealed. Moths in the genus *Schizura* display many shades of red, chocolate, green, and teal blue, all of which can be found in one specimen. The elegant prominent, *Odontosia elegans* (pl. 28), is mostly brown—but probably over two hundred shades of brown that blend delicately from soft cream, through rich orange-beige, all the way to an exquisite chocolate. It truly is an elegant moth that challenges the notion that brown is not colorful. Before I started working with moths I shared in the preconception that many of them were not that colorful. Now, after having really seeing them up close, there is not a single species that I would consider to be dull and uninteresting.

Not all moths rest tent-like, or with their wings folded down over their bodies. Many species have adopted some postures that help them with camouflage or impersonate features in their environment as a defense mechanism. One of the oddest impersonations, by the genus *Lithacodia* and the species *Cerma cerintha* of the family Noctuidae (pls. 35, 36, 37), involves the imitation of bird-droppings. They do this through a remarkable combination of color and pattern as well as shifts in the size of their scales across their wings and body. The underwing moths of the genus *Catocala* in the Noctuidae have forewings that readily blend into tree bark where they rest during daylight hours. Once startled they flash a brightly colored hind wing that may range across yellows, oranges and reds, as with *Catocala ilia conspicua* (pl. 42), to scare predators away. *Catocala relicta* (pl. 41) forgoes a brightly colored underwing and mimics the coloration of aspen and poplar tree barks as a simple but effective mottled black-and-white camouflage. The use of ocular spots on hind wings is yet another curious defense mechanism. The Io moth, *Automeris io* (pls. 10, 11), and the Sphinx moth species, *Smerinthus jamaicensis* (pl. 5), have spots that they keep covered when at rest but flash when they are startled. The appearance of what seems to be the large eyes of a much larger animal often succeeds in confusing an attacker.

The dizzying diversity of moths generates such a vast array of choices that it becomes problematic to select a group of them and create an exhibition. When I mount exhibitions of my works, I remain quite aware of the play of color and form across the walls, so I ensure that no two shows have ever been alike. I prefer presenting my prints in large clusters where they appear tightly grouped together. In this manner the diversity of moths becomes more evident. Even though each image contains an enormous amount of visual information, placing images next to each other attracts the viewer in such a way that it is difficult to see any single species as the most important.

The images in this book were selected from thousands of scans. An exhibition of the prints in this book would take up an enormous amount of space, and so the book format has provided me with new opportunities. I hope that by creating this collection of images I can show the vastness of moth bio-diversity as well as the unique design of individual species, and ultimately that I will create a greater appreciation for this amazing group of insects.

Moths: Species Rich, but Little Known

Marc Epstein

The number of named moth species is estimated at around 150,000, roughly eight times the number of butterflies. As the number of moths that remain to be described is far greater than for butterflies, this discrepancy will grow. Tropical regions have the highest numbers of species, (and are thus sometimes referred to as species rich). However, a lighted sheet in a temperate forest at night will also attract a surprising bounty of moths. In the order Lepidoptera, moths rule in terms of quantity, but relatively little is known about them, in particular by the general public.

Moths can display a tremendous amount of variation in wing color, shade, and pattern, even within local populations. This can make them very difficult to identify. The wing patterns may grade from one extreme to another or be rather fixed, locally or regionally. Polymorphism refers to the presence of distinct forms, such as melanics, in a local population. Often it can be difficult to determine whether one is looking at the same species unless you have access to a large collection of specimens.

From the pages of this book you will get a sense of the variety of wing shapes and patterns, as well as the different body forms found in moths.

A closer look reveals wings and bodies covered with scales of different shapes and sizes. Many of the antennae are feathery, while others are not. Here you will be able to see the amount of detail that normally would only be possible with the aid of microscopes or good hand lenses. The diversity of wing types reflects a combination of aerodynamics as well as the postures of the species at rest (while most of the moths in this book are night flyers, moths have to perch somewhere during the day). Other moths are noted for defenses that purportedly scare off predators. These include brightly colored or eye-spotted hind wings that are hidden by forewings when the moth is at rest. During an attack the hind wing is exposed, startling the vertebrate predator. Mimetic color patterns, better known in butterflies, also occur in moths. These include clearwing wasp mimics, complete with striped abdomens and legs, as well as patterns that ape unpalatable butterflies and other insects, such as cockroaches. Some moths even have forewings that resemble snakes in appearance. Crypsis, or the ability to be disguised, is another important defense. Patterns that blend with leaves and bark are common in moths, in particular in geometrids. Some moths, such as acontiine noctuids, resemble bird droppings. Another defense utilized by major moth groups is the ability to evade bats. This is achieved through their hearing structure, or tympanum, which detects the squeaks that bats use in echo-location.

Differences occur within species in the size of moths of the same sex, as well as in their wing shape. This can be due to genetic or environmental influences. Female moths are typically larger than the males, with more rounded forewings. Since both are not always seen together, there are other means needed to tell them apart. Distinguishing male and female moths can at times be as simple as telling a comb-like (or pectinate) antenna from a threadlike antenna. However, this is not always the case. For one thing, male moths have a wide diversity of antennal types. The male giant silk moths famously sport a broad comb, while the female has a much narrower antenna. This is often true in limacodid moths as well; however, limacodids include interesting examples that have broad, pectinate antenna in both males and females. This has led to mistakes in the original descriptions of species, which were thought to be males but were later found to be the opposite sex. Female moths laden with eggs can also be distinguished from their male counterparts by a round, distended abdomen. Extreme differences between males and females, particularly in the wings, are referred to as sexual dimorphism.

There are examples in which the males have wings and the females are flightless, either with wings (e.g. gypsy moth) or without wings (e.g. cankerworm). In such cases, associating the males and females of the same species can be very difficult. It is frequently not until moths have been reared from the same group of like caterpillars that this has been determined.

Some of our best observations of moths show how they react to a light source and then how they rest near the source. Illuminating a white sheet that is stretched on a line with ultraviolet, fluorescent, or mercury vapor light is an excellent method for observing the diversity of moths and their behavior. There are certain moths that visit the light soon after dusk, while others are not seen until the wee hours of the morning; some come directly to the light, while others approach the illuminated area, but keep a certain distance, either away from the sheet entirely or alighting some distance from the light. Perhaps the most fascinating things to observe about moths are their unusual resting postures. One can easily be fooled into thinking there is a small piece of wood stuck on the sheet. Wings are folded in a myriad of ways: for example, closed over the back, spread out horizontally or held more closely forming a bell-shaped silhouette below the body. The abdomens, particularly of males, can be curled, or in pyraloids the brush-like ends can be seen to move from side to side.

There is one popular explanation for moths' attraction to light and flames. In the nocturnal moth's world of locating a mate or finding a suitable plant to lay eggs, the moon is said to act as a navigation device. Thus in nature the moth's light source is normally distant rather than close. If they fly at an angle to the distant source of light moths do not reach the light, but encounter a plume of pheromone or the scent of a plant and are diverted. An alternative explanation is that moths are actually trying to escape from the light source, but are fooled by a misinterpretation of the light—they see the middle of the source as darkness. In general, male moths come to lights in greater numbers than females, though there are certainly exceptions. Some species of nocturnal moths are not attracted to lights, or at least the lights commonly used to attract them (for example, ultraviolet or mercury vapor).

So far we have focused on the adult stage of moths, however our personal introduction to moths often begins with the discovery of a caterpillar, which we raise to the adult stage. While the vast majority of caterpillars feed on terrestrial plants or detritus, there are also carnivorous or parasitic caterpillars that live off other insects. There are even caterpillars that are fully aquatic. Caterpillars utilize silk in diverse ways. Young caterpillars can be dispersed in the wind, using their silk strands like ballooning spiders. Bagworms and case-bearers use silk to construct a moveable protective cover

Estigmene acrea

over the larva and eventual pupa. Tent caterpillars live in group-constructed shelters, as do others such as the fall webworm. The most familiar caterpillars feed externally on leaves; others roll or tie leaves, mine a leaf internally, or bore inside stems or trees. The caterpillars of clothes moths (best known as household pests) feed on keratinous material in the wild, including carrion. Numerous caterpillars spin cocoons and subsequently become pupae inside these silken structures. However, there are many species, such as those of sphinx moths, which burrow in the ground and become pupae without a cocoon.

The observation of adult sphinx moths gives us a classic example of moth feeding, as they hover at dusk, their lengthy proboscuses extended into floral tubes. Clearwing sphinxes drink nectar in broad daylight, but many other moths can be observed nectaring at night simply by shining a flashlight on flowering bushes. In the tropics sphinxes in the genus *Aellopos* can be seen taking a quick airborne sip from a puddle on the road. Many moths are active liquid feeders, much like their butterfly brethren. Some moths prefer to feed on sap or rotten fruit, and one way to attract them is with a technique called sugaring. If one takes a slightly fermented "brew" (molasses, fruit, beer, etc.) and paints it on tree trunks, certain moths will come to imbibe. In temperate climates underwing moths, of the genus *Catocala* in particular, are known to be attracted to this food. Some noctuid moths will pierce skin, using their proboscuses to suck animal blood, while others are fruit-piercing, or both. Giant silk moths do not take nectar or other nutrients, as their mouth parts are reduced. They are able to live and produce eggs from the body fat amassed during the caterpillar stage.

Lepidoptera are classified in families, like other animals or plants. A superfamily is a collection of families believed to have common origin. Knowledge of superfamily characteristics is a wise first step to understanding moths. This includes recognizing the general appearance of both the adult and immature stages (the eggs, caterpillars, and pupae). Learning the biologies of the families and superfamilies, although often very diverse, is also an important stage in grasping their classification. Superfamily names are based on the name of a family that occurs within it. The largest Lepidoptera superfamilies, in order of the numbers of described species, include the Noctuoidea, with over 40,000, followed by Geometroidea and Pyraloidea, each with over 20,000. The Papilionoidea (butterflies), if grouped with related superfamilies (skippers and heydyloids), and Gelechioidea are each over 15,000, with the number of the tiny gelechioids expected to rival the second or third largest groups of Lepidoptera. The next group of the largest superfamilies includes Tortricoidea (tortrix moths) at about 9,000 described species. Bombycoidea (silk moths and sphingids) and Tineoidea (including the clothes moths) each have around 4,000 or more species, followed by Zygaenoidea (burnet moths and slug caterpillars), Gracillarioidea, and Yponomeutoidea (ermine moths).

Pachysphinx modesta

Furcula borealis

Atteva punctella

In the genealogy of Lepidoptera, butterflies and most of the moth families are in a group called the Ditrysia. Ditrysia and a few more primitive families as well are said to be heteroneurous. This means that the veins on the forewings are different from those on the hind wings. The lower, more primitive groups, once referred to as the Monotrysia, are no longer considered a group with a common ancestor. Many of these primitive families, which make up less than one percent of the total species of Lepidoptera, are said to be homoneurous, having fore- and hind wings with roughly the same veins.

Finally one question most frequently asked of entomologists is how to tell moths from butterflies. The problem is that there are many exceptions to the standard answers, some anatomical and others behavioral. Moreover, the best scientific evidence has few reliable features that cannot be easily observed, for example the idea that butterflies are diurnal and moths are nocturnal. While this is true of most butterflies, there are many day-flying moths, including those of the Arctiidae (tiger moths). An aspect of the wings can often separate butterflies from moths: the majority of moths have a spine (males) or spines (females) at the base of the leading edge of the hind wing called a frenulum. This hooks into a latch at the base of the forewing called the retinaculum.

This mechanism effectively holds the wings together during flight and at rest. Butterflies do not have a frenulum, relying instead on a large humeral lobe on the base of the hind wing's leading edge. That butterflies have clubs on the end of their antennae is also often cited as a way of distinguishing them from moths. Once again, there are many moth examples of this feature, particularly in day-flying castniids and zygaenids, as well as in noctuids. Ultimately it is perhaps best to think of butterflies as being one of several experiments in the evolution of day-flying in Lepidoptera, the species overwhelmingly dominated by beautiful but little-understood moths.

This book provides a unique opportunity to understand the wonder of moths. Its large images provide a new experience, a new vision akin to a patchwork quilt. It allows the viewer to see details that have previously only been visible through a stereomicroscope, though even then a microscopic view of a large moth under the lowest magnification does not allow one to see an entire wing. While a vast amount of new information on moths awaits our discovery, I believe that this book will bring the rich diversity of moths to a new audience, while providing those already interested in moths with captivating images.

Further Reading

Covell, Charles V. Jnr., *Eastern Moths: Peterson Field Guides.* Boston: Houghton Mifflin, 1984 (o/p).

Holland, W.J., *The Moth Book, A Popular Guide to a Knowledge of the Moths of North America*, New York: Dover Publications, 1903/1968 (o/p).

Miller, Jeffrey C., and Paul C. Hammond, *Macromoths of Northwest Forests and Woodlands*, Morgantown, West Virginia: U.S. Department of Agriculture, Forest Service, Forest Health Technology Enterprise Team (FHTET-98-18), 2000.

Tuskes, Paul M., James P. Tuttle, and Michael M. Collins, *The Wild Silk Moths of North America.* Ithaca and London: Comstock Publishing Associates, 1996.

Wagner, D.L., V. Giles, R.C. Reardon, and M.L. McManus, *Caterpillars of Eastern Forests*, Morgantown, West Virginia: U.S. Department of Agriculture, Forest Service, National Center of Forest Health Management (FHTET-96-34), 1997.

Moth Clubs: The Lepidopterists Society, c/o Kelly Richers, Asst. Treasurer, 9417 Carvalho Court, Bakersfield, CA 93311, USA.

Hydriomena perfracta

Nature's Art and Technological Visions

Johanna Drucker

The moths are startling to behold. The remarkable fullness of their presence takes us by surprise. They appear with hallucinatory intensity in these super-charged graphic images whose hyper-realism surpasses photographic accuracy, approaching the threshold of the uncanny. Looming monsters, fantastic machines, exotic creations of an unnaturally exaggerated nature, Joseph Scheer's moths produce a sensation of wonder about the seemingly inexhaustible splendor of the world. We almost forget, looking at these prints, that these are not moths, but their simulacral phantom trace, created by techniques as complex as the subjects represented.

The archives of natural history are filled with images provoked by science and answered by art. Every such image provides evidence of the sensibility of its time as well as the skill of an individual artist. Visual perception organizes experience into a graphic record according to models that are always historically as well as individually inflected. An artist not only draws, but literally sees, according to the frameworks of visual knowledge that prevail at any given moment. Vision has an independent history that intertwines with the genealogy of methods and styles of representation. Whether they are unique, autographic works or editioned prints, images involve many levels of translation. The extra mediation imposed by printmaking only multiplies the steps in already elaborate processes of interpretation.

Production media add their own filters into the way visual experience is encoded and communicated. When we look at these striking images, the extreme detail and fineness of resolution contribute inordinately to our sense that the specimens have been made present almost without mediation. The scaled, furry bodies of these amazing creatures seem to have been transmitted through a recording process that simply, merely, miraculously transcends all the mediating effects of traditional nature drawing by means of a technology so transparent it leaves hardly a trace of its translation in the image. Nothing, however, could be further from the truth.

The technological apparatus of modern digital scanners is merely one in a continuous line of prosthetic devices by which naturalists have peered with determined curiosity at the wonders of the natural world. Artists and scientists have long been intent on extracting from their own observations the fullest possible account of the phenomena before their eyes, but they rely on all kinds of technology to do so. Anton von Leeuwenhoek, staring through his primitive 17th-century microscopes—barely more than mounted lenses capable of adjusting their distance from a hapless specimen stuck on a pin to keep its wiggling within viewing range—is Scheer's predecessor in one aspect of this undertaking. When Leeuwenhoek named the amazing creatures he perceived in specimens of dental plaque and saliva "wee beasties", he was not simply contributing to knowledge, he was inventing new categories within which knowledge itself could be conceived. And when his contemporary, Robert Hooke, produced his remarkable publication *Micrographia* in 1665, he added to the sum of human visual understanding a set of drawn models through which that hitherto unknown world could be grasped.

Vision and knowledge are bound together in the material of images. For the history of science is a record of conjurings, a pyramid of reliable knowledge schemes in which the handmaid of the visual arts helps to build the consensual model according to which our sense of the world is constructed. That order of things is continually reinvented: in some epochs merely shifted by degrees, and in others revolutionized. Every image has a place within that order, either reinforcing its familiar notions or pushing us in some imaginative way towards an unexpected insight. Scheer's moth prints show us an inspired way of seeing. They are artworks, not scientific records. They do not offer a glimpse of a system of knowledge *about* the world so much as they delight *in* the world as available to sensual, perceptible experience.

The capacity of visual images to create believable records of scientific and naturalistic inquiry is intimately bound up with the history of reproductive technology. In Antiquity, Pliny bemoaned the inaccuracy of visual images. Their creation depended upon the skills of hand and eye, and an idiosyncratic talent; and then even the best efforts would have to suffer new distortions as they were hand-copied for circulation. The need for standardized and repeatable images as a base for shared knowledge arguably held the advancement of science back for centuries. Not until wood-block and copper engraving became viable media of communication did the discourse of science begin to move from its dependence upon the more stable, if otherwise ambiguous, system of verbal description into an expanded discourse of word and image relations.

Art historian William Ivins, in his landmark *Prints and Visual Communication* of 1953, proposed the oft-cited phrase, "exactly repeatable visual statement" to describe the images made possible by print technology. The boon to Renaissance science provided by such images was indisputable. The wood-block drawings that illustrate an herbal of the *Pseudo-Apuleius* printed in Rome in 1483 are crudely lacking in the detail that made the prints in the German publication *Gart der Gesundheit* seem so accurate by contrast when produced just a few years later. The former were derived almost entirely from earlier images, already much debased by being several times removed from

original observation of plant specimens, while the latter had been drawn anew. Once they were put into circulation, the descriptive accuracy of these images raised the bar for standards of presentation. The skills' base in producing printed records of visual, particularly natural, phenomena rose as a result of the circulation of such exemplary models.

The notion of what constitutes verisimilitude is subject to intellectual fashion. Ideas about what something *should* look like are changed by what it *can* look like given technological, artistic, and conceptual skills. The obstacles to direct representation reside as much in the filtering effects of a culturally shaped perception as they do in the ability of metal or wood to reproduce accurately a record of what has been perceived. Famous images of beached whales studied close-up exhibit the sharp teeth of monstrous creatures unknown in the cetaceous universe. Why? Because the cognitive model of what was to be seen so over-determined the process of supposedly empirical observation that attributes of the beast's morphology were exaggerated or distorted to make them align with expectations.

Agrius cingulata

Of course the great mythic turning point in such trajectories is supposed to belong to the advent of photographic representation. In 1844 William Henry Fox Talbot elegantly described the camera as a "pencil of nature"—as if the instrument merely and directly inscribed the light that fell directly on a receptive surface bearing a solution of salts that darkened in response. From the outset this image suggested that photography is the most uncoded of media. Such a notion is open to much critical debate. From its invention, the status of photography as an art depended on the struggle to allow for individual expressivity in its use. At the same time as its status as a truth-bearing medium resided in its ability to produce images that passed for apparently unmediated records. As late as the 1960s, the critically sophisticated French semiotician, Roland Barthes characterized photography as a "message without a code," as if the technical device of lenses, mirrors, exposure times, film granularity and speed, were all incidental rather than material and substantive elements of photographic image production.

Geina tenuidae

Photography is an expressive medium as surely as the autographic modes of drawing, painting, etching, engraving, or lithography. But photography, by its nature, seems disposed to a directness that no hand-produced image can approach. Transparency, the idea of pure visual information, depends on the idea that one can successfully minimize the distorting effects of individual subjectivity or the interpretive cast of an artist's eye in the process of image production. The popular conception of photography bears this out, as is evident in the habitual verbal constructions that we use in discussing such pictures. "This is a luna moth," the phrase; but "this" is not a luna moth—it is an image resulting from a highly sophisticated set of procedures enabled by electronic processing of digitally encoded information and a set of output devices. An elaborately produced print from a digital file made on a flat-bed scanner at a particular resolution uses specific software capable of capturing and processing information according to carefully calibrated parameters.

But to say that is to undermine the other important feature of the works of Joseph Scheer and of the place his images occupy within a longer aesthetic trajectory. From the Renaissance to the present the naturalist artist is served by the continual improvement of the technological means of production and reproduction. Less obviously, but just as importantly, the vision of artists has informed the sciences and the broader culture within which

scientific knowledge comes to have its current credibility. The artistry of vision, the conceptual imagination and leaps that spring from creative imagination, have to be appreciated as a part of the cultural history within which Scheer's work is placed. Insufficient to imagine that the artist's view of nature is always only subservient to a naturalist's agenda, or constrained by the needs of a community of scientists. Were that so, the sciences, as well as the arts, would suffer stagnation. For the ability of artists to see through new media to the beyond of what was not formerly available to perception is as essential to the creation of new cultural knowledge in visual form as is the apparatus. The technology does not make the art any more than the science does, and the visual imagination that springs from the inner eye is what pushes the cognitive models to engage afresh with perceptual experience. The dialogue of mediated representation and human understanding is a continual back and forth exchange between leaps of visual faith and the effective means of making a believable display of knowledge.

The naturalist artist offers a contrast to the fine artist. John James Audubon (1785–1857) or the botanical illustrator Maria Sibylla Merian (1647–1717) were artists who pushed their observation of natural phenomena to the highest level of aesthetic investigation. But the discipline of natural history has always regarded images as dependent upon a textual field for stability. A gloss in the dependable medium of language anchors these images, saving them from the perils of ambiguity or obscurity. Named, labelled, and identified, they are safely linked to a system of classification within which their visual forms are able to fulfill the ancillary role of fleshing out the identity of the specimen for study and future identification. But in the world of fine art, most emphatically in the modern era, visual images have declared their independence from the literary and the linguistic. The naturalist pioneer for this, the daring Joseph Le Moyne de Morgues, made watercolor studies of animals and plants in the 1880s that had no textual apparatus to support them. Like his contemporaries among the Impressionist and Realist painters of the period, he asserted the visual primacy of images.

Insistence on the capacity of images to simply be, rather than represent, became a bromide of the early 20th-century theorists of fine art. The insistence on the presence of visual forms as immediately available to the eye became so integrated into our sense of what an artwork is that it has colored the contemporary audience expectation that any visual or sculptural artifact should be understandable just by looking. This exaggerated, even caricatured, idea of the innocent eye (for the artist or the viewer) belies the complex apprenticeship by which acculturated beings acquire any kind of cognitive understanding. But the other side to such assertions is more profound, and more relevant to our appreciation of Scheer's undertaking. For the ability of visual models of knowledge to form primary documents of understanding is reliant on our willingness to engage with the specific properties of imagery as a means of encoding and communicating according to particular models of intellectual insight. Coupled with this is a keen need to appreciate the qualities of the individual media into which such insight is inscribed.

Scheer's work combines trajectories of the naturalist scientist who opens a world of visual knowledge and understanding with the artist's impulse to see first and intellectualize afterwards. Seeing and knowing inform each other. Art is a way of researching new knowledge, and of showing the means by which such knowledge can be created. Following the track of the incidental impulse is crucial in such work. The moths that landed on Scheer's scanner came almost by accident, as part of a sweep of miscellany he subjected to the process of scanning, processing, and output. A printmaker by training and disposition, Scheer was exploring the capacities of new tools to extend his own aesthetic reach.

An elaborate set of studio skills and equipment are necessary to produce the illusion of transparency these images possess. The scanners, capable of resolutions of 14,000 pixels per inch, are optical information-gathering devices of unparalleled power. The Iris printers that displaced Scheer's earlier lithographic print production are industry tools whose first, fugitive inks have been replaced by archival quality pigments. The programs for image processing that permit stochastic screens to be used in the separation process are generated algorithmically, rather than mechanically, and the fine-grained variation of the effects has a subtle reality that is distinct from the rigid repetition that traditional half-tones communicate to the eye. Huge racks of storage in hard drives and external media are needed to hold files of mega-, giga-, and tera-byte dimensions. The production apparatus required for these images is of industrial caliber, and in the axiom of production economics, they disappear all the more completely, absorbed into the product. Labor also disappears, as do the demanding tasks of artistic process. The image reifies its subject, turning the dynamic beauty of these haunting flying machines into stopped specimens, objectified and fixed in the technological gaze. Artistry, deft skill in craft and performance, seems absent, even as it finds expression using sophisticated tools.

But the technology is only an instrument, and Scheer's moth prints are indisputably fine art. The optical scanners he uses extend visual processing capability, registering light as information so that it can be manipulated as data. The images generated from these files can readily conform to photographic conventions equated with visual realism— so much so that the bodies of these moths appear to have almost passed directly through the apparatus and into an image. But that effect is a result of aesthetic persuasiveness achieved through technological assistance, rather than the result of some automated mechanism. If they seem almost more real than the moths themselves, that is because they are possessed of a greater rhetorical potency than the original specimens. The artist's hand and studio skills—arranging, touching, re-touching at each stage—are integral to the decision-making processes in these works. When we turn our gaze back to the world with those images before our eyes, we are ready to extend their richness to the experience of perceptible life, aware that many other marvels might be conjured through the sensibility at work in Scheer's new millennial atelier.

Further Reading
Roland Barthes, *Image, Music, Text* (NY: Hill and Wang, 1973).
Ann Shelby Blum, *Picturing Nature* (Princeton: Princeton University Press, 1993).
William M. Ivins, Jr., *Prints and Visual Communication* (Cambridge: Harvard University Press, 1953).
Estelle Jussim, *Visual Communication and the Graphic Arts* (NY: Bowker, 1983).
Peter Galison, http://www.hosting.zkm.de/icon/stories/story Reader$14

Night Visions

1 *Laothoe juglandis* (male)

2   *Laothoe juglandis* (female)

3 *Pachysphinx modesta*

4 *Paonias excaecatus*

5 _Smerinthus jamaicensis_

6   *Agrius cingulata*

7 *Hemaris thysbe*

11 *Automeris io* (female)

12 *Dryocampa rubicunda*

13   *Pyrrharctia isabella*

14   *Spilosoma virginica*

15 *Estigmene acrea*

16 *Antheraea polyphemus*

17 *Hyalophora cecropia*

18   *Grammia virgo*

19 *Grammia virguncula*

20   *Apantesis phalerata*

21 *Apantesis nais*

22 *Arctia caja americana*

23 · *Halysidota tessellaris*

24   *Lophocampa caryae*

25 *Lycomorpha pholus*

26 *Holomelina laeta*

27   *Hypoprepia fucosa*

28 *Odontosia elegans*

29   *Nadata gibbosa*

30 *Haploa clymene*

31 *Noctua pronuba*

32 *Cisseps fulvicollis*

33 *Ctenucha virginica*

34   *Anaplectoides prasina*

35 *Lithacodia concinnimacula*

36 *Lithacodia carneola*

37 *Cerma cerintha*

Plusia putnami

39 *Schizura badia*

40 *Oligia bridghami*

41   *Catocala relicta*

42   *Catocala ilia conspicua*

43   *Magusa orbifera*

44   *Zanclognatha laevigata*

45 *Habrosyne scripta*

46   *Heliomata cycladata*

47   *Eudeilinia herminiata*

48   *Furcula borealis*

49   *Plagodis kuetzingi*

50   *Plagodis fervidaria*

51   *Caripeta angustiorata*

52　*Ennomos magnaria*

53   *Metanema inatomaria*

54   *Nemoria mimosaria*

55   *Dyspteris abortivaria*

Hydriomena perfracta

57   *Cnaemidophorus rhododactylus*

58   *Hellinsia species*

59 *Geina tenuidactyla*

60 *Eurrhypara hortulata*

61   *Pantographa limata*

62   *Vaxi auratella*

63   *Crambus agitatellus*

64   *Chrysoteuchia topiaria*

65   *Hypsopygia costalis*

66   *Sparganothis unifasciana*

67   *Lithacodes fasciola*

68   *Euclea delphinii*

69 *Trichotaphe flavocostella*

70   *Zeuzera pyrina*

71   *Yponomeuta multipunctella*

72 *Atteva punctella*

LIST OF MOTHS

Dimensions refer to the wingspan

Sphinx Moths are members of the family **Sphingidae**, and are medium to very large in size. Many have a long proboscis and feed at flowers, hence they sometimes are confused with hummingbirds. Some fly and feed during the day; others fly only at dusk or at night. The caterpillars feed on many kinds of woody and herbaceous plants, and pupation usually occurs in soil or loose, leaf litter without a cocoon. Elongated powerful wings make these moths very fast fliers. The common name "sphinx" comes from the behavior of the larvae who rear up mimicking the pose of the mythical creature. The caterpillars often have a long, slender horn on the back near the end of the body, thus giving them the common name "hornworm."

Ceratomia undulosa (waved sphinx)
Subfamily Sphinginae
Size: 10.4 cm

Paonias excaecatus (blinded sphinx)
Subfamily Sphinginae
Size: 9 cm
Plate 4

Sphinx kalmiae (laurel sphinx)
Subfamily Sphinginae
Size: 9.8 cm

Laothoe juglandis (male) (walnut sphinx)
Subfamily Sphinginae
Size: 7 cm
Plate 1

Paonias myops (small-eyed sphinx)
Subfamily Sphinginae
Size: 7.5 cm

Sphinx luscitiosa (Clemen's sphinx)
Subfamily Sphinginae
Size: 7.8 cm

Laothoe juglandis (female) (walnut sphinx)
Subfamily Sphinginae
Size: 7.3 cm
Plate 2

Smerinthus cerisyi (one-eyed sphinx)
Subfamily Sphinginae
Size: 8.2 cm

Darapsa myron (Virginia creeper or grapevine sphinx)
Subfamily Macroglossinae
Size: 6 cm

Agrius cingulata (pink-spotted hawk-moth)
Subfamily Sphinginae
Size: 11.2 cm
Plate 6

Pachysphinx modesta (modest sphinx)
Subfamily Sphinginae
Size: 11.6 cm
Plate 3

Smerinthus jamaicensis (twin-spotted sphinx)
Subfamily Sphinginae
Size: 7 cm
Plate 5

Darapsa pholus (azalea sphinx)
Subfamily Macroglossinae
Size: 6.5 cm

Deidamia inscripta (lettered sphinx)
Subfamily Macroglossinae
Size: 7 cm

Hemaris thysbe (hummingbird clearwing)
Subfamily Macroglossinae
Size: 5.4 cm
Plate 7

Hyles gallii
(bedstraw hawk-moth)
Subfamily Macroglossinae
Size: 6.7 cm

Hyles lineata (white-lined sphinx)
Subfamily Macroglossinae
Size: 9 cm
Plate 8

Giant silk moths are members of the family **Saturniidae**, and they are some of the largest and showiest of all moths; hence they are widely collected and raised from caterpillars. Some pupate in well-built silken cocoons and others in a cell in the soil. Some caterpillars such as those of *Automeris io* have sharp stinging hairs. Giant silk moth caterpillars feed on the leaves of trees and shrubs. Adult moths do not feed, having a vestigial proboscis. They live off body fat stored during the caterpillar phase. Families related to the Saturniidae include Bombycidae (silk moths), Sphingidae, Lasiocampidae, and Mimallonidae.

Dryocampa rubicunda (rosy maple moth)
Subfamily Citheroniinae
Size: 5.5 cm
Plate 12

Automeris io (male)
Subfamily Hemileucinae
Size: 7 cm
Plate 10

Automeris io (female)
Subfamily Hemileucinae
Size: 8 cm
Plate 11

Actias luna
Subfamily Saturniinae
Size: 10.8 cm
Plate 9

Antheraea polyphemus
Subfamily Saturniinae
Size: 10.8 cm
Plate 16

Hyalophora cecropia
Subfamily Saturniinae
Size: 10.8 cm
Plate 17

Tent caterpillars or lappet moths are members of the family **Lasiocampidae**. These are medium-sized moths with hairy bodies. Their colorful striped larvae often live in groups, constructing webbed tents to protect themselves from predators. The moths pupate in a silken cocoon, some of which have been used to make cloth. They feed on foliage of deciduous trees and shrubs and can cause major defoliation.

Malacosoma disstria
(forest tent caterpillar)
Family Lasiocampidae
Size: 3 cm

Phyllodesma americana
(lappet moth)
Family Lasiocampidae
Size: 4.2 cm

Tolype velleda (large tolype)
Family Lasiocampidae
Size: 4.8 cm

Tiger moths are members of the family **Arctiidae**, and are colorful small to medium-sized moths. This family also includes the lichen and wasp moths. The tiger moth's bright colors warn predators that it is poisonous. Some also make clicking sounds that bats recognize, thus avoiding them because of their foul taste. Because the larvae are usually hairy, members of the subfamily Arctiinae are known as woolly bears. The larvae feed on many kinds of herbaceous and woody plants, as well as lichens. They pupate in cocoons made of matted larval hair with little or no silk. The adults may be diurnal or nocturnal fliers. Many arctiids also have the common name of tussock moth. This causes confusion with the like-named species in the gypsy moth's family (Lymantriidae).

Sack bearers are members of the family **Mimallonidae**. They are medium-sized hairy moths. The adults have an unusual resting posture, with all four wings visible and held below the body. The larvae are thick in the middle and taper towards the ends. Late instars build open-ended cases or sacks of silk and leaves. The scalloped sack-bearer feeds on oaks.

Arctia caja americana (great tiger moth)
Subfamily Arctiinae
Size: 6.8 cm
Plate 22

Estigmene acrea (salt marsh/acrea moth)
Subfamily Arctiinae
Size: 5.5 cm
Plate 15

Apantesis phalerata (harnessed tiger moth)
Subfamily Arctiinae
Size: 4 cm
Plate 20

Grammia virgo (virgin tiger moth)
Subfamily Arctiinae
Size: 6.2 cm
Plate 18

Apantesis nais (Nais tiger moth)
Subfamily Arctiinae
Size: 3.7 cm
Plate 21

Grammia virguncula (little virgin tiger moth)
Subfamily Arctiinae
Size: 4.3 cm
Plate 19

Lacosoma chiridota
(scalloped sack-bearer)
Family Mimallonidae
Size: 3.6 cm

Lycomorpha pholus (black and yellow lichen moth)
Subfamily Lithosiinae
Size: 3.1 cm
Plate 25

Cycnia tenera
(delicate cycnia/dogbane tiger moth)
Subfamily Arctiinae
Size: 4 cm

Halysidota tessellaris
(banded tussock/pale tiger moth)
Subfamily Arctiinae
Size: 4.4 cm
Plate 23

Haploa clymene (clymene moth)
Subfamily Arctiinae
Size: 5.1 cm
Plate 30

Lophocampa caryae (hickory tussock moth)
Subfamily Arctiinae
Size: 4.3 cm
Plate 24

Cisseps fulvicollis (yellow-collared scape moth)
Subfamily Ctenuchinae
Size: 3.4 cm
Plate 32

Acronicta innotata
(unmarked dagger moth)
Subfamily Acronictinae
Size: 3.5 cm

Holomelina laeta (joyful holomelina)
Subfamily Arctiinae
Size: 2.6 cm
Plate 26

Phragmatobia fuliginosa
(ruby tiger moth)
Subfamily Arctiinae
Size: 5 cm

Ctenucha virginica (Virginia ctenuchid)
Subfamily Ctenuchinae
Size: 5 cm
Plate 33

Harrisimemna trisignata
(Harris's three-spot)
Subfamily Acronictinae
Size: 3.8 cm

Holomelina immaculata
(immaculate holomelina)
Subfamily Arctiinae
Size: 3 cm

Pyrrharctia isabella
(isabella tiger moth/banded woolly bear)
Subfamily Arctiinae
Size: 3.4 cm
Plate 13

Owlet moths are members of the family **Noctuidae**, which is the largest family of Lepidoptera in number of species. Their size ranges from small to very large with the majority being medium in size. The larvae feed on a wide range of foliage plants as well as dead leaves, lichens, and fungi. A few species are leaf miners and some feed in rolled leaves; others bore into stems, roots, or fruits. Some feed on scale insects or other caterpillars in addition to leaves. Cutworms hide in leaf litter during the day and bite off tender plant shoots at night. Pupation occurs in cells in the soil, in cavities in the food plant, or in silken cocoons that may include parts of the food plant. This family is divided into 29 subfamilies.

Agrotis subterranean
(subterranean dart)
Subfamily Noctuinae
Size: 4 cm

Hypoprepia fucosa (painted lichen moth)
Subfamily Arctiinae
Size: 2.5 cm
Plate 27

Spilosoma virginica
(Virginian tiger moth/yellow bear moth)
Subfamily Arctiinae
Size: 5.2 cm
Plate 14

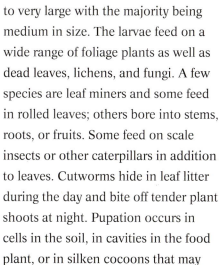

Anaplectoides prasina (green arches)
Subfamily Noctuinae
Size: 5 cm
Plate 34

Eueretagrotis perattenta
(two-spot dart)
Subfamily Noctuinae
Size: 3 cm

Callopistria mollissima
(pink-shaded fern moth)
Subfamily Amphipyrinae
Size: 2.6 cm

Papaipema arctivorens (northern burdock borer)
Subfamily Amphipyrinae
Size: 3.6 cm

Leuconycta diphteroides
(green Leuconycta)
Subfamily Condicinae
Size: 3.5 cm

Noctua pronuba (greater yellow underwing)
Subfamily Noctuinae
Size: 4.7 cm
Plate 31

Euplexia benesimilis
(American angle shades)
Subfamily Amphipyrinae
Size: 3.3 cm

Phlogophora iris
(olive angle shades)
Subfamily Amphipyrinae
Size: 5 cm

Lithacodia carneola (pink-barred Lithacodia)
Subfamily Eustrotiinae
Size: 2.3 cm
Plate 36

Metaxaglaea inulta
(unsated sallow)
Subfamily Cuculliinae
Size: 4.5 cm

Magusa orbifera (orbed narrow-wing)
Subfamily Amphipyrinae
Size: 4.2 cm
Plate 43

Eudryas grata
(beautiful wood nymph)
Subfamily Agaristinae
Size: 4.5 cm

Lithacodia synochitis
(black-dotted Lithacodia)
Subfamily Eustrotiinae
Size: 2 cm

Apamea amputatrix
(yellow-headed cutworm)
Subfamily Amphipyrinae
Size: 5 cm

Oligia bridghami (Bridgham's brocade)
Subfamily Amphipyrinae
Size: 3 cm
Plate 40

Cerma cerintha (tufted bird-dropping)
Subfamily Acontiinae
Size: 3.1 cm
Plate 37

Lithacodia concinnimacula (red spotted Lithacodia)
Subfamily Eustrotiinae
Size: 2.4 cm
Plate 35

Autographa mappa
Subfamily Plusiinae
Size: 4 cm

Plusia putnami (Putnam's looper)
Subfamily Plusiinae
Size: 3.5 cm
Plate 38

Parallelia bistriaris
(maple looper)
Subfamily Catocalinae
Size: 4.7 cm

Prominents are members of the family **Notodontidae** and are medium-sized stout-bodied moths. At rest the wings are held roof-like or rolled over the body making them look like small twigs or sticks. Larvae vary greatly in appearance and many have unusual shapes. The normally fleshy abdominal prolegs at the end of the body form a thin tail or are modified into glands. Larvae eat leaves of many trees, over-winter, and then pupate in the spring in a cell in the soil or in a loose cocoon on the ground.

Diachrysia aeroides
Subfamily Plusiinae
Size: 3.9 cm

Catocala ilia conspicua (ilia underwing)
Subfamily Catocalinae
Size: 7.7 cm
Plate 42

Bomolocha baltimoralis
(Baltimore Bomolocha)
Subfamily Hypeninae
Size: 3.4 cm

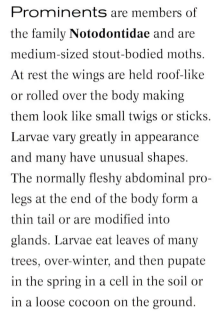

Diachrysia balluca
Subfamily Plusiinae
Size: 5 cm

Catocala relicta (white underwing)
Subfamily Catocalinae
Size: 8 cm
Plate 41

Palthis angulalis
(dark-spotted Palthis)
Subfamily Herminiinae
Size: 2.5 cm

Dasylophia thyatiroides
(gray-patched prominent)
Family Notodontidae
Size: 4.8 cm

Megalographa biloba
(bi-lobed looper)
Subfamily Plusiinae
Size: 4.4 cm

Catocala lacrymosa
(tearful underwing)
Subfamily Catocalinae
Size: 7.8 cm

Zanclognatha lacvigata
Subfamily Herminiinae
Size: 2.7 cm
Plate 44

Ellida caniplaga
(linden prominent)
Family Notodontidae
Size: 4.5 cm

Furcula borealis (white furcula)
Family Notodontidae
Size: 4 cm
Plate 48

Macrurocampa marthesia (green form)
(mottled prominent)
Family Notodontidae
Size: 5.1 cm

Peridea ferruginea
(chocolate prominent)
Family Notodontidae
Size: 4.5 cm

Schizura ipomoeae
(morning glory prominent)
Family Notodontidae
Size: 4.4 cm

Heterocampa biundata
(wavy-lined heterocampa)
Family Notodontidae
Size: 5 cm

Nadata gibbosa (white-dotted prominent)
Family Notodontidae
Size: 5.1 cm
Plate 29

Schizura unicornis (red form)
(unicorn caterpillar moth)
Family Notodontidae
Size: 3.6 cm

Schizura leptinoides
(black-blotched schizura)
Family Notodontidae
Size: 4.1 cm

Hyperaeschra georgica
(georgian prominent)
Family Notodontidae
Size: 4.4 cm

Odontosia elegans (elegant prominent)
Family Notodontidae
Size: 5.8 cm
Plate 28

Schizura unicornis
(unicorn caterpillar moth)
Family Notodontidae
Size: 3.9 cm

Hook-tip moths are members of the family **Drepanidae**. The apex of the forewing is often hooked, as the name suggests, except for the species in the genus *Eudeilinea*. The caterpillars feed on many trees and shrubs, in loosely rolled leaves, and pupate in cocoons in leaf litter. Larvae lack prolegs on the end of the abdomen. The moths in the subfamily Thyatirinae are medium-sized, with broad wings similar to the owlet moths and prominents except for their wing venation.

Macrurocampa marthesia
(mottled prominent)
Family Notodontidae
Size: 5 cm

Oligocentria semirufescens
(red-washed prominent)
Family Notodontidae
Size: 4.5 cm

Schizura badia (chestnut schizura)
Family Notodontidae
Size: 3.5 cm
Plate 39

Eudeilinia herminiata (northern eudeilinia)
Subfamily Drepaninae
Size: 2.7 cm
Plate 47

Habrosyne scripta (lettered habrosyne)
Subfamily Thyatirinae
Size: 3.5 cm
Plate 45

Pseudothyatira cymatophoroides
(tufted thyatirid)
Subfamily Thyatirinae
Size: 4.5 cm

Geometer moths are members of the family **Geometridae**. Other common names are inchworm or measuring-worm moths. They are small to medium-sized with broad wings and slender bodies. This family has the second largest number of named species within the Lepidoptera. They feed on numerous herbaceous and woody plants. Larvae usually have the first three pairs of abdominal prolegs missing and move by extending the front of the body as far forward as possible and then looping the rear up to meet the front legs. This unusual gait gives them their common name. They pupate in loose cocoons in leaf litter or in the soil.

Campaea perlata (pale beauty)
Subfamily Ennominae
Size: 4.5 cm

Caripeta angustiorata (brown pine looper)
Subfamily Ennominae
Size: 3 cm
Plate 51

Ennomos magnaria (maple spanworm)
Subfamily Ennominae
Size: 5.5 cm
Plate 52

Eufidonia notataria
(powder moth)
Subfamily Ennominae
Size: 2.2 cm

Heliomata cycladata (common spring)
Subfamily Ennominae
Size: 2 cm
Plate 46

Lomographa vestaliata
(white spring)
Subfamily Ennominae
Size: 2.5 cm

Metanema inatomaria (pale metanema)
Subfamily Ennominae
Size: 2.8 cm
Plate 53

Plagodis alcoolaria
(hollow-spotted Plagodis)
Subfamily Ennominae
Size: 3.1 cm

Plagodis kuetzingi (purple plagodis)
Subfamily Ennominae
Size: 2.7 cm
Plate 49

Plagodis fervidaria (fervid Plagodis)
Subfamily Ennominae
Size: 2.4 cm
Plate 50

Plagodis serinaria (lemon Plagodis)
Subfamily Ennominae
Size: 3.7 cm

Dyspteris abortivaria (bad wing)
Subfamily Larentiinae
Size: 2.2 cm
Plate 55

Plume moths are members of the family **Pterophoridae**. They are mostly small moths with long slender legs. At rest the wings are rolled in a T-shape at right angles to its body. The forewing is deeply notched and the hindwing is divided into three fringed lobes resembling plumes. Larvae are leaf rollers or borers.

Hellinsia species
Family Pterophoridae
Size: 2.6 cm

Tetracis crocallata (yellow slant-line)
Subfamily Ennominae
Size: 4 cm

Eupithecia ravocostaliata
Subfamily Larentiinae
Size: 1.9 cm

Cnaemidophorus rhododactylus
Family Pterophoridae
Size: 2.1 cm
Plate 57

Geina tenuidactyla
Family Pterophoridae
Size: 1.1 cm
Plate 59

Nacophora quernaria (melanic form) (oak beauty)
Subfamily Ennominae
Size: 5.2 cm

Hydria prunivorata (Ferguson's scallop shell)
Subfamily Larentiinae
Size: 3 cm

Emmelina monodactyla
Family Pterophoridae
Size: 2.4 cm

Grass moths are members of the subfamily Crambinae in the family **Crambidae**. They are medium-small to small moths with little forewing pattern, often streaked with silver or metallic colors. Their long, narrow forewings are often rolled to resemble twigs when the moth is at rest. Larvae are webworms, stem borers, or leaf rollers, attacking turf grasses, sugar cane, and a variety of trees. The subfamily Pyraustinae has adults that can be either brightly or cryptically colored. The subfamily Nymphulinae has aquatic larvae, complete with gills.

Nemoria mimosaria (white-fringed emerald)
Subfamily Geometrinae
Size: 2 cm
Plate 54

Hydriomena perfracta
Subfamily Larentiinae
Size: 2.8 cm
Plate 56

Hellinsia species
Family Pterophoridae
Size: 2.2 cm
Plate 58

Crambus agitatellus
Subfamily Crambinae
Size: 1.8 cm
Plate 63

Eurrhypara hortulata
Subfamily Pyraustinae
Size: 2.3 cm
Plate 60

Euzophera ostricolorella (root collar borer)
Subfamily Phycitinae
Size: 3.4 cm

Euclea delphinii (spiny oak slug moth)
Family Limacodidae
Size: 2.3 cm
Plate 68

Chrysoteuchia topiaria
Subfamily Crambinae
Size: 1.6 cm
Plate 64

Vaxi auratella
Subfamily Crambinae
Size: 1.5 cm
Plate 62

Pyralid moths are members of the family **Pyralidae**, and are small to medium-sized moths. Larvae are usually concealed when feeding. Some roll leaves or form webs, while others bore into plants. Some are scavengers of organic matter, feed on scale insects, or live in the nests of bees or other Hymenoptera. The Indian meal moth is a cosmopolitan pest attacking stored food products in the home.

Slug and nettle caterpillars are members of the family **Limacodidae**. The moths are medium to medium-small in size. The caterpillars have a translucent undersurface formed from reduced and modified prolegs. The names slug and nettle caterpillar come from the different types of dorsal surfaces of the larvae. The slug, or gelatine, type is smooth or granulated, often well camouflaged. The nettle type has spiny warts, or scoli. The cocoons are often ovoid and hard, with a lid that pops off when the adult emerges.

Lithacodes fasciola
Family Limacodidae
Size: 2 cm
Plate 67

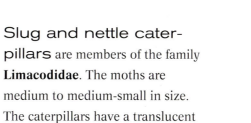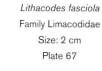

Packardia geminata
Family Limacodidae
Size: 2.1 cm

Pantographa limata (basswood leaf roller)
Subfamily Pyraustinae
Size: 3.4 cm
Plate 61

Hypsopygia costalis (clover hayworm moth)
Subfamily Pyralinae
Size: 1.4 cm
Plate 65

Apoda biguttata
Family Limacodidae
Size: 2.4 cm

Tortricidia flexuosa
Family Limacodidae
Size: 1.5 cm

Tortricidia testacea
Family Limacodidae
Size: 1.7 cm

Proteoteras moffatiana
Subfamily Olethreutinae
Size: 1.6 cm

Argyrotaenia velutinana (redbanded leafroller)
Subfamily Tortricinae
Size: 1.2 cm

Carpenter, leopard or goat moths are members of the family **Cossidae**. The adults vary from small to very large, with wing venation that is considered to be primitive among the Ditrysian moths. The caterpillars are internal feeders and bore into trees or roots, where they can live four years or more. The wichity grub of Australia is the larvae of a very large cossid moth, measuring almost 20 cm.

Leaf roller, tortrix, or bell moths are members of the family **Tortricidae**. The moths are small to medium-small in size. At rest they hold their forewings flat, forming a bell-like silhouette. The caterpillars can be orchard or forest pests as leaf tiers or rollers (Tortricinae), or root, stem or fruit borers (Olethreutinae). The codling moth is a well-known apple pest, and the spruce budworm is an important pest of conifers. Some larvae bore into seeds, and the Mexican Jumping Bean is an example of this behavior. Pupation occurs in loose shelters or under bark.

Olethreutes species
Subfamily Olethreutinae
Size: 1.4 cm

Clepsis persicana (white-triangle Tortix)
Subfamily Tortricinae
Size: 1.6 cm

Eucosma tocullionana (white pine cone borer)
Subfamily Olethreutinae
Size: 1 cm

Sparganothis unifasciana
Subfamily Tortricinae
Size: 1.8 cm
Plate 66

Zeuzera pyrina (leopard moth)
Family Cossidae
Size: 4.4 cm
Plate 70

Epiblema scudderiana
Subfamily Olethreutinae
Size: 1.7 cm

Cydia latiferreana (filbert worm moth)
Subfamily Olethreutinae
Size: 2.2 cm

Eulia ministrana
Subfamily Tortricinae
Size: 1.8 cm

Clear-winged moths are members of the family **Sesiidae**, and are medium to small in size. The largely transparent forewings and hindwings make these easy to identify. Larvae are borers in many herbaceous and woody plants, and some are serious pests in garden and fruit crops. The majority are day fliers (although the species in this book is not), and they often mimic wasps.

Synanthedon acerni (maple callus borer)
Family Cossidae
Size: 1.8 cm

Ermine moths are members of the family **Yponomeutidae**, and are medium to small moths. Some species have dotted forewings and rest with their wings rolled to resemble sticks. Larvae live communally in webbing spun over food plant leaves, where they pupate.

Atteva punctella (Ailanthus webworm)
Family Yponomeutidae
Size: 2.5 cm
Plate 72

Yponomeuta multipunctella (American ermine moth)
Family Yponomeutidae
Size: 2 cm
Plate 71

Gelechiid moths are members of the family **Gelechiidae**, and are small to very small in size. They are characterized by long, slender labial palps, upturned like an elephant's tusks. Larvae feed widely in diverse ways as leaf miners, folders and tiers. They may form stem galls as well as feed in fruit and seeds.

Trichotaphe flavocostella
Family Gelechiidae
Size: 1.5 cm
Plate 69

Case-bearer moths are members of the family **Coleophoridae**, and are small to very small, with lance-like wings. Larvae are miners in leaves, seeds and sometimes stems. They form portable cases from frass, plant material, and silk.

Coleophora deauratella
Family Coleophoridae
Size: 1 cm

Oecophorid moths are members of the family **Oecophoridae**. They are very small to medium-sized moths. Larvae feed in concealed webs or in rolled or tied leaves. Some feed on dead animal carcasses or fungi. Pupation takes place in the larval shelters, in other parts of the food plant, or in the soil.

Antaeotricha leucillana
Family Oecophoridae
Size: 1.8 cm

Author's Acknowledgments

It would have never been possible to produce my current work or such a beautiful book were it not for the support of many friends, colleagues, and organizations. I would like to express my deepest appreciation to them all.

It was Stephen Hulburt's enthusiastic response that ignited the initial spark. Jürgen Tesch, publisher at Prestel, shared my desire for a large-format book and convinced me to work with Prestel. I am most grateful for having had the opportunity to work with Philippa Hurd, the editor, in assembling the text and planning the content of the book. I could not have hoped for a more elegant design for this collection than Meike Sellier's achievement. Their insights and suggestions make it a much more compelling book than it would have otherwise been. I want to thank Johanna Drucker not only for her introduction that places my work in a historical context, but also for all the intense conversations that allowed me to benefit from her critical perspective for a number of years. Marc Epstein's encouragement, enthusiasm, and criticism have been invaluable to me. I am grateful for his friendship and his introductions to members of the scientific community. His contributions to this book help generate a clearer understanding of the very complex life-histories and diversity of moth families. The responsibility for the identification of the moths represented in this book, including possible errors, falls to me. However, this would not have been possible without the help of a number of scientists whom I consulted on the difficult cases. I am indebted to the following specialists who took time to either confirm or correct the identification of, and in some cases directly identify, species from images sent to them: John Brown, Mike Pogue and Alma Solis (Systematic Entomology Laboratory, USDA), Jean-Francois Landry (Agriculture and Agri-Food Canada), Tim McCabe (New York State Museum), William Miller (University of Minnesota), Paul Opler (Colorado State University), and Reed Watkins (Crumpton, Maryland). Manuscript suggestions by John Brown, Mike Pogue, and David Wagner (University of Connecticut) were also very valuable.

It is important for me to acknowledge the New York State Council for the Arts, the Experimental Television Center in Owego, New York, and Alfred University for funding my art/research and the team at Creo Inc. for supporting the technology that I use. Without their generosity this project would have never happened. A special thanks goes to my Dean, Richard Thompson, for supporting leave that allowed me to dedicate the necessary time to this project.

The support of a number of individuals has been crucial to the development of my work. I have shared vision and friendship with the Co-Founders and Co-Directors of The Institute for Electronic Arts, Peer Bode and Jessie Shefrin. Our former Dean, David Pye's, belief in us was crucial in bringing our vision to fruition. I would like to recognize the kindness and support that I continually receive from Nat and Erin Dickinson, Xiaowen and Yuan Chen, Pam Joseph, Robert Brinker, and Gerar Edizel. Finally, I want to thank Mark Klingensmith for the enthusiasm he brings to our collaboration and to the members of his family, Kasey, Allister, and Isaac, all of whom participated in unique ways.

This book is dedicated to my parents, James and Kathleen Scheer, for all their loving support.

Front and back cover: *Grammia virgo* (see pl. 18).
Frontispiece: *Campaea perlata* (see p. 115); *Diachrysia balluca* (see p. 113).
Contents: *Hyalophora cecropia* (see pl. 17).

Prestel Verlag
Königinstrasse 9, D-80539 Munich
Tel. +49 (89) 38 17 09-0
Fax +49 (89) 38 17 09-35
www.prestel.de

Prestel Publishing Ltd.
4, Bloomsbury Place, London WC1A 2QA
Tel. +44 (020) 7323 5004
Fax +44 (020) 7636 8004

Prestel Publishing
175 Fifth Avenue, Suite 402,
New York, N.Y. 10010
Tel. +1 (212) 995-2720
Fax +1 (212) 995-2733
www.prestel.com

Library of Congress Control Number: 2003107834

The Deutsche Bibliothek holds a record of this publication in the Deutsche Nationalbibliographie; detailed bibliographical data can be found under: http://dnb.dde.de

Prestel books are available worldwide.
Please contact your nearest bookseller or one of the above addresses for information concerning your local distributor.

Editorial direction: Philippa Hurd
Design and layout: Meike Sellier, Munich
Origination: Reproline Genceller, Munich
Printing and binding: ebs, Verona

Printed in Italy on acid-free paper.

ISBN 3-7913-2968-5